Novels for Students, Volume 31

Project Editor: Sara Constantakis Rights Acquisition and Management: Jennifer Altschul, Margaret Chamberlain-Gaston, Leitha Etheridge-Sims, Kelly Quin Composition: Evi Abou-El-Seoud Manufacturing: Drew Kalasky

Imaging: John Watkins

Product Design: Pamela A. E. Galbreath, Jennifer Wahi Content Conversion: Katrina Coach Product Manager: Meggin Condino © 2010 Gale, Cengage Learning

For product information and technology assistance, contact us at **Gale Customer Support, 1-800-877-4253.**

For permission to use material from this text or product, submit all requests online at **www.cengage.com/permissions.**

Further permissions questions can be emailed to **permissionrequest@cengage.com** While every effort has been made to ensure the reliability of the information presented in this publication, Gale, a part of Cengage Learning, does not guarantee the accuracy of the data contained herein. Gale accepts no payment for listing; and inclusion in the publication of any organization, agency, institution, publication, service, or individual does not imply endorsement of the editors or publisher. Errors brought to the attention of the publisher and verified to the satisfaction of the publisher will be corrected in future editions.

Gale
27500 Drake Rd.
Farmington Hills, MI, 48331-3535

ISBN-13: 978-1-4144-4169-6
ISBN-10: 1-4144-4169-X
ISSN 1094-3552

This title is also available as an e-book.
ISBN-13: 978-1-4144-4947-0
ISBN-10: 1-4144-4947-X
Contact your Gale, a part of Cengage Learning sales
representative for ordering information.

Printed in the United States of America
1 2 3 4 5 6 7 14 13 12 11 10

The Namesake

Jhumpa Lahiri 2003

Introduction

Jhumpa Lahiri's second book, *The Namesake*, was published in the United States in 2003. The book was well received by critics and highly anticipated. This anticipation was based on Lahiri's first book, the Pulitzer prize-winning collection of short stories titled *Interpreter of Maladies*. Like its predecessor, *The Namesake* explores issues of the Indian American immigrant experience and the corresponding anxieties of assimilation (conforming) and exile. From these themes of dual nationality, the question of identity arises, and this theme is further underscored by the main character's dual names. The strength of familial bonds in the midst of this cultural quandary is also addressed.

To this end, *The Namesake* portrays the Ganguli family over a course of thirty-two years. It follows Ashoke and Ashima Ganguli from shortly after their emigration from Calcutta, India, to Cambridge, Massachusetts, in the late 1960s. The story then follows the couple as their children are born and raised in the United States. It is their struggles, particularly those of the eldest son, Gogol, that comprise the bulk of the story. Notably, the novel's deft and sensitive handling of the immigrant experience has caused it to be featured in school curriculums throughout the United States.

Author Biography

Jhumpa Lahiri was born Nilanjana Sudeshna Lahiri in London, England, on July 11, 1967. However, she was raised in South Kingstown, Rhode Island. (The name under which Lahiri lives and writes was in fact a nickname bestowed upon her by a grade-school teacher). Lahiri is the eldest daughter of Amar K. Lahiri, a professor at the University of Rhode Island, and Tapati Lahiri, a teacher. Lahiri began writing stories at a young age, though she did not pursue a writing career while she was in college. Indeed, after earning her B.A. from Barnard College, she intended to continue her graduate studies. However, Lahiri's applications were not initially accepted, and she instead began working as a research assistant. It was around this time that she began writing again, before going on to study creative writing at Boston University. At that university, she earned three master's degrees, in English, creative writing, and comparative literature. She also received her Ph.D. in Renaissance studies there. Then, rather than continue her academic career, Lahiri devoted herself to writing, publishing her work in such periodicals as the *New Yorker* and the *Harvard Review*.

Several of these early stories appear in Lahiri's first book, the 1999 collection *Interpreter of Maladies*. The volume was an instant bestseller, launching Lahiri into the international spotlight. Among several accolades, the collection won the

Pulitzer Prize for fiction in 2000. The following year, Lahiri married newspaper editor Alberto Vourvoulias-Bush. (The couple has since had two children.) In 2003, Lahiri released her first novel, *The Namesake*, and in 2008, she published her second collection of short stories, *Unaccustomed Earth*. The latter was awarded the Commonwealth Writers' Prize in 2009. Indeed, with so few books to her credit, Lahiri's fame and renown are remarkable. Her work has been read the world over, and it is best known for its autobiographical nature, largely reflecting Lahiri's own Indian American heritage.

Plot Summary

1.

1968

Ashima Ganguli is nearly nine months pregnant with her first child. She is in her apartment in Cambridge, Massachusetts. Her husband, Ashoke, is studying for his doctorate in engineering in the next room. Ashima's labor begins, and the couple takes a taxi to the hospital. After Ashima has checked in, Ashoke leaves her there and promises to return. Ashima has been in the United States for a year and a half, leaving Calcutta immediately following her arranged marriage to Ashoke. Alone at the hospital, Ashima is afraid to raise her child in America. By four o'clock the following morning, Ashima has reached the final stages of her labor, and Ashoke returns to the hospital, where he sits in the waiting room.

He paces and thinks of the fateful train accident that has brought him to this moment. As an undergraduate student in India, Ashoke had been on a train on his way to visit his grandfather. There, he met a businessman who had traveled the world, returning to India only because his wife was homesick. The man told Ashoke that returning was his greatest regret, and he urged Ashoke to travel. Shortly afterward, while Ashoke was rereading

Nikolai Gogol's "The Overcoat," a favorite short story by his favorite author, the train crashed. The businessman beside him was killed, and Ashoke lay immobile in the wreckage with the torn and crumpled pages of his book. When the rescuers arrived, they noticed him only because the pages were moving in the breeze. It was a year before he was able to walk again, and during his long recovery, Ashoke thought constantly of the businessman's advice. Seven years have passed and he still credits Nikolai Gogol for saving his life.

2.

The baby is a boy. All of the Bengali friends Ashima and Ashoke have made gather at the hospital to greet him. The baby has not been named because the Gangulis are waiting for a letter from Ashima's grandmother. The letter contains the names she has picked for her grandchild, one for a boy and one for a girl. The letter was sent over a month ago, but it still has not arrived. After three days in the hospital, Ashima and the baby are ready to go home, but they must fill out the birth certificate and choose a name before leaving. They name the baby Gogol as an homage to Ashoke's life-changing accident. The name will be a pet name, they decide, a practice common in India. Both Ashoke and Ashima have pet names. In school, at work, and in public, they are addressed by their formal names, but at home, family members call one another by their pet names. Unfortunately, the letter never arrives. Ashima's grandmother has had a stroke, and Gogol's intended formal name has been irrevocably lost.

At first, Ashima struggles with motherhood. She is tired, sad, and homesick. However, she soon adjusts to her new routine, enjoying her renewed purpose and the attention of strangers who stop to talk to her and admire the baby. When Gogol is six months old, the Gangulis invite their Bengali friends over for his *annaprasan*, a ceremony in which Gogol is fed his first solid food. In addition, he is presented with a dollar, a pen, and soil. Whichever the baby chooses will foretell his career as either a businessman, a scholar, or a landowner. Gogol refuses all three.

3.

1971

The Gangulis have moved to a suburb just outside Boston, Massachusetts. Ashoke is working as an assistant professor at a nearby university. Although Ashoke loves his job, Ashima hates their suburban surroundings. In fact, the move from Cambridge to the suburbs was harder on her than the move from Calcutta to Cambridge. Now that Gogol is almost four years old, he is going to day care a few days a week. Without Gogol to care for, Ashima once again finds herself bored. Two years later, the family buys its first home, a newly built ranch in Pemberton, Massachusetts. The house has not yet been landscaped, and Gogol's earliest memories are of playing in the dirt.

When Gogol is five, Ashima learns she is pregnant. Now that Gogol is about to begin kindergarten, his parents finally choose a formal name for him, Nikhil. This name, too, is chosen in honor of Nikolai Gogol, the author of the short story Ashoke was reading during the accident. Gogol, however, has become accustomed to his pet name, and he does not wish to be called Nikhil. His American teachers do not understand the Indian tradition of pet and formal names; his birth certificate lists his name as Gogol and the boy refuses to answer to Nikhil. Thus, his teachers call him Gogol despite his parents' wishes.

Media Adaptations

- An unabridged audio adaptation of *The Namesake*, narrated by Sarita Choudhury, was released by Random House in 2003.

- *The Namesake* was adapted as a film

with the same title in 2006. Directed by Mira Nair and produced by Fox Searchlight, this fairly literal adaptation is widely available on DVD.

Gogol's sister is born the following May. His parents name her Sonali, forgoing the pet and formal names because of the confusion they have caused for Gogol. Her name eventually becomes shortened to the more Americanized "Sonia." At her annaprasan, Sonia chooses the dirt and tries to eat the dollar bill. A guest at the party laughs and says, "This one is the true American."

The years go by. Ashoke is tenured and both sets of parents in India pass away one by one. Although the family visits Calcutta every few years, they have become more and more Americanized, even celebrating Easter and Christmas. The children prefer American food to Indian food. Gogol even resents taking classes in Bengali language and culture because he would rather be at his drawing class.

4.

1982

It is Gogol's fourteenth birthday. His family throws an American birthday party for him and his school friends and then a Bengali party for the family's friends. After the second party, Ashoke gives Gogol a book of Nikolai Gogol's short stories. It is the first gift the boy has ever received directly from his father (all the others having been picked by Ashima and given in Ashoke's name). Gogol feigns interest, but he has long since grown to hate his name and namesake. He resents its oddity, neither Bengali nor American. He does not know the story behind his name. In fact, Ashoke is about to tell his son the story, but something about Gogol's reticence makes him hesitate. After Ashoke leaves the room, Gogol sets the book on a shelf without even opening it.

A year later, Ashoke is up for sabbatical from his university position, and the family decides to take an extended trip to India, a trip both Gogol and Sonia resent. For them, America is their home, not Calcutta. For their parents, it is the reverse. After they return, Gogol's junior year of high school commences and he studies his namesake in English class. Though he is supposed to read "The Overcoat," Gogol does not do so. "To read the story, he believes, would mean paying tribute to his namesake, accepting it somehow." As high school wears on, Gogol does well, though he occasionally sneaks out with his friends to go to concerts in Boston. On one such outing, he attends a college party. He meets a girl there but dreads telling her his name; once again having to face the usual questions that arise from its telling. This time, he says his name is Nikhil. She comments that Nikhil is a beautiful name, and the two kiss before the night is out.

5.

Gogol is now eighteen and about to attend Yale University, a prestigious school in New Haven, Connecticut. Before doing so, he goes to the courthouse alone and has his name legally changed to Nikhil. His parents begrudgingly accept their son's decision. Gogol tells the judge that he hates his current name, that he's "always hated it." Despite his name change, everyone he knows continues to call him Gogol. It is not until he begins his new semester at Yale that he truly comes into his own as Nikhil. Nevertheless, it takes a long time for him to "feel like Nikhil." His dual names—one at school, one at home—make him feel as if "he's cast himself in a play acting the part of twins." Stranger still is when his parents visit him at school and call him Nikhil. However, when his mother forgets and calls him Gogol, her mistake also feels strange. Gogol "feels helpless, annoyed … caught in the mess he's made."

Gogol begins to feel more at home at school than in Pemberton. He continues to draw and begins sketching buildings, ultimately majoring in architecture. Headed home for Thanksgiving on the train during his sophomore year, Gogol meets Ruth, another Yale student. They fall in love, but Gogol does not mention her to his parents. After a year has gone by, Gogol has met Ruth's parents and been accepted by them. Ruth has not met Ashoke and Ashima. Even though Gogol's parents have since become aware of the relationship, they disapprove of it. Later, Ruth spends a year studying in England.

Although the couple maintains a long-distance relationship, they ultimately grow apart and break up soon after Ruth returns.

For Thanksgiving break of his senior year, Gogol heads home on the train once more. Ashima and Sonia are in India attending a cousin's wedding, so Ashoke will pick Gogol up from the station alone. In Rhode Island, someone commits suicide by jumping in front of the train, and thus Gogol is late arriving home. Ashoke has been waiting and worrying at the station for several hours. On the drive home, Ashoke finally tells Gogol about the train accident he was in as a young man, about the true meaning of his son's name. Gogol is shocked but relieved to know the truth. When Gogol asks his father if he is a reminder of the accident, Ashoke replies, "You remind me of everything that followed."

6.

1994

Since graduating from Yale, Gogol has moved to New York City and earned his graduate degree from Columbia University. He has begun working at an architectural firm. One night at a party, he meets Maxine Ratliff. She lives with her parents in a mansion in Chelsea, a neighborhood in New York City (though she has an entire floor of the house to herself). On their first date, they have dinner at the house with Maxine's parents. The family regularly dines on fine food and wine. Their lifestyle embodies an effortless, distinctly American gentility that Gogol aspires to. As he falls in love with Maxine, he also falls in love with her family and their lifestyle.

Eventually, Maxine invites Gogol to move in with her. Gogol often thinks of the vast differences between his family and hers; "he is conscious of the fact that his immersion in Maxine's family is a betrayal of his own." As with Ruth, Gogol waits as long as possible before mentioning Maxine to his parents. He eventually introduces her, and despite Gogol's fears, the visit goes well. Maxine likes his parents and is not embarrassed by their Indian-ness, although Gogol is.

Maxine, her parents, and Gogol enjoy a summer vacation at the Ratliff's lake house in New Hampshire. Again Gogol thinks of how his parents would never fit into the genteel Ratliff family. They celebrate Gogol's twenty-seventh birthday at the lake, inviting the other families who live around the lake. One partygoer makes an ignorant remark about Gogol's heritage. He is forced to remind her and, to his surprise, Maxine's mother that he was born and raised in America. That night, Gogol is surprised that his parents have not called him to wish him a happy birthday, but later he realizes he never gave them the phone number at the lake house and that the number is not listed. Gogol feels relieved by the realization that his family cannot reach him, and that relief makes him think "that here at Maxine's side, in this cloistered wilderness, he is free."

7.

Ashoke is working as a visiting professor in Cleveland, Ohio, but Ashima has chosen to remain in Pemberton. With Sonia having long since moved to California, Ashima, for the first time in her life, is living alone. She does not like it, and she begins working part-time at the library to fill her days. Ashoke flies home for short visits every third weekend. One Sunday afternoon, Ashima is alone preparing the family Christmas cards. Ashoke calls her and says that he has driven himself to the emergency room with a stomachache; his regular doctor's office is closed. He tells her not to worry and says he will call her later.

The hours pass and Ashima grows increasingly worried. She finally calls the hospital and is told that Ashoke has died of a heart attack. Ashima is shocked. In New York, Gogol learns that his mother called while he was out but decides to call her back tomorrow. Then Sonia calls and tells him the news. Gogol flies to Cleveland the next day to retrieve his father's body, and although Maxine offers to go with him, he prefers to go alone. In Cleveland, Gogol also wraps up his father's affairs. He returns to the house in Pemberton a day later.

The surviving Gangulis are often surrounded by their Bengali friends, but they eat a mourner's diet when they are alone. That diet consists of blandly cooked vegetables and lentils. Gogol remembers being annoyed by this ritual when he was younger, but now he clings to it. This marks a major change in Gogol's outlook. On the eleventh day following Ashoke's death, a ceremony is held to mark the end of the mourning period. Maxine also attends. This time, Gogol is not embarrassed by his family or their customs. In fact, her presence there seems odd to him. Maxine wants to know when Gogol will return to the city, and she asks about a vacation they had planned. She says they need to get away, but Gogol says he does not want to escape. This also marks a major change in his outlook.

Throughout that December, Gogol, Sonia, and Ashima live together in the house in Pemberton. Sonia decides to move back from California and attend law school in Boston. Gogol returns to New York on the train, though now he returns home to visit every weekend.

8.

A year after Ashoke's death, Gogol is no longer seeing Maxine; she eventually tired of his growing attachment to his family and her exclusion from that part of his life and is engaged to another man. Gogol continues to visit Pemberton regularly, and Sonia is living with Ashima. Ashima has always been the family chef, but now Sonia now does all the cooking. Ashima has grown frail and listless. Gogol begins taking classes to prepare for his architectural licensing exam. He meets and begins an affair with Bridget, a married woman. It is a cold liaison that does not last long, ending when

Gogol begins to feel guilty about the affair.

As time goes by, Ashima nags Gogol about settling down and starting a family. She finally convinces him to go on a date with Moushumi Mazoomdar, the daughter of old family friends. In fact, Gogol and Moushumi attended the same sprawling Bengali parties as children, though they never interacted. She is a doctoral student at New York University. Both are surprised by how well their first date goes, and they agree to meet again. Again to their mutual surprise, they fall in love. Their similar backgrounds bond them; both rejected their heritage, and yet they resented their American lovers for doing the same.

9.

Less than a year after their first date, Moushumi and Gogol plan to marry. Although both would prefer a small American wedding, they give in to their families and have a large Bengali ceremony. Gogol has just turned thirty, and his wedding is another reminder of his father's absence. The couple takes the money they receive as wedding gifts and puts it toward a new apartment.

The two postpone their honeymoon because of Moushumi's teaching schedule, but they travel together to Paris when Moushumi is invited to attend a conference there. She is fluent in French, having lived and studied in Paris, and the inequity between her familiarity with Paris and Gogol's unfamiliarity is starkly apparent. It seems to hint at a chasm between them.

One spring, Gogol and Moushumi are at a dinner party, one of the frequent gatherings held by Moushumi's college friends. Most of her friends are professors, artists, or editors. Gogol does not care for these affairs but goes because Moushumi cares very deeply about them. He knows she wants her life to resemble the lives of her friends (just as Gogol used to wish his family's life resembled the Ratliffs'). The party's hosts are expecting their first child, and the conversation turns to baby names. This has been a recurring conversation at almost every dinner party Gogol and Moushumi have attended lately. Gogol is exceedingly bored by the topic; however, this particular night, Moushumi reveals Gogol's given name to their friends, an act he resents. He tells the group that he believes children should be allowed to choose their own names when they are eighteen. The other partygoers, and even his wife, stare at Gogol incredulously.

10.

1999

Gogol and Moushumi celebrate their first anniversary. Although Moushumi still loves Gogol, she has become somewhat distant. Their dinner does not go well. Moushumi finds it to be too expensive, too fussy. She leaves hungry and sad.

On her way to teach her last class before

completing her doctorate, Moushumi finds herself in the university's mailroom. There, she comes across the résumé of an old flame, Dimitri Desjardins. She writes down his contact information and calls him a week later. They begin an affair, and Mousshumi spends Monday and Wednesday evening with Dimitri before returning to sleep at home with Gogol. Dimitri is middle aged, balding, and unemployed; his apartment is in disarray. Gogol does not suspect a thing.

11.

Moushumi leaves alone for a conference in Palm Beach, Florida, although Gogol would have preferred to join her. She says she will have too much work to do there, but he sees her pack a bathing suit. Gogol works through the weekend, looking forward to Moushumi's return. But he also thinks of the previous week, when he and his wife hosted Thanksgiving dinner. Sonia brought her new boyfriend, Ben, and their love presented a disappointing contrast to Gogol and Moushumi's relationship. Thinking of Moushumi's growing distance, Gogol decides they need a vacation, and he plans a trip to Italy for the coming spring. The trip will be a surprise Christmas gift.

12.

2000

A year later, Ashima is preparing to throw a

Christmas party, the last that will be held in the Pemberton house. The house has just been sold, and she plans to spend six months a year in Calcutta with relatives and the other six months in the United States visiting her children and family friends. She has grown into an independent woman, no longer afraid to live and travel alone. Though she has spent over three decades missing India, she knows that she will miss America. It has become as much a part of her as her birthplace. Sonia and Ben are engaged, and she knows that "he has brought happiness to her daughter, in a way Moushumi had never brought to her son." Ashima even feels guilty for having nagged her son to date Moushumi in the first place.

Gogol arrives on the train. He thinks of his mother's travel plans and of his parents' bravery in living so far from their home. He thinks of how little he has seen of the world, and of how he has always lived a short train ride from Pemberton. He also thinks of the same train ride a year ago, when he discovered Moushumi's affair. It was "the first time in his life [when] another man's name upset him more than his own." Moushumi moved out immediately, returning to Paris, and she and Gogol divorced a few months later. The following spring, Gogol traveled alone to Italy, taking the trip he had initially planned as a surprise for his wife.

Back at the party, Gogol breaks away and heads to his old room. He packs a few boxes of his old books. He discovers the volume of Nikolai Gogol's short stories, the long-forgotten gift from his father. Opening it for the first time, Gogol finds an inscription from Ashoke, and it causes Gogol to realize that "the name he had so detested ... was the first thing his father had ever given him." He also thinks that there are only a few people left in his life who know him as Gogol rather than Nikhil; "yet the thought of this eventual demise provides no sense of victory, no solace. It provides no solace at all." Gogol opens the book and begins to read.

Characters

Ben

Ben is introduced in the second half of the novel as Sonia's boyfriend. He eventually becomes Sonia's husband. Ben makes Sonia happy, a fact that both Gogol and Ashima acknowledge. Ben acts as a contrast to Moushumi, who has failed to make Gogol happy.

Dimitri Desjardins

Dimitri Desjardins is the man with whom Moushumi has an affair. The two originally met when Moushumi was in high school and Dimitri was in college. At that time, the two had struck up a pseudo-romantic relationship that lasted off and on for several years, yet that relationship was never consummated. When Moushumi later comes across Dimitri's résumé, she secretly contacts him and finds that he has become a balding, unemployed, middle-aged man with a sad apartment. Nonetheless, she begins an affair with him.

Ashima Ganguli

Ashima is Ashoke's wife and the mother of Gogol and Sonia. She represents the traditional Indian values and lifestyle that Gogol grows to resent. Indeed, Ashima adored living in India with her sprawling family. She worked as an English tutor before entering into an arranged marriage with Ashoke. In their entire married life together, Ashima never addressed her husband directly as Ashoke, a reflection of Indian tradition. After her arrival in America, Ashima is extremely homesick; she is afraid to raise her child in America without the support of her family. However, over time, she grows accustomed to her life in America, even celebrating Christmas and Easter for her children. Still, Ashima cooks predominantly Indian food and visits India every few years. She also maintains her roots by practicing Hindu rituals and making predominantly Bengali friends. These Bengali friends become something of a surrogate extended family for Ashima. The raucous parties she throws for her Bengali friends punctuate the Ganguli family's life over the course of three decades.

When Ashoke is working in Cleveland, Ashima lives alone for the first time in her life, a frightening experience for her. Once again, though, she shows her inner strength and adaptability by getting a part-time job, her first job since before she was married. Through this job, Ashima makes the first truly American friends she has ever had. When Ashoke suddenly dies, Ashima grows frail and listless, and it is a long while before she adjusts to her widowhood. By the story's end, however, Ashima has grown independent enough to sell the family home and travel back and forth between India and America. The latter country, she knows, has become as much a part of her now as her birthplace.

Ashoke Ganguli

Ashoke is Ashima's husband and the father of Gogol and Sonia. Ashoke is a rather stoic and reserved individual who plays the traditional role of distant father and breadwinner. In most cases in the book, he is referred to as being at work. Ashoke's deeper nature, however, is revealed through his love of Russian literature. His deeper nature is also revealed through his life-changing encounter with the businessman who urges him to travel and the subsequent train accident. It is further revealed through Ashoke's subsequent rescue, a rescue that hinges on the crumpled pages of a story by Nikolai Gogol. This incident influences Ashoke's life and the name he chooses for his son. Although Ashoke is a rather static (unchanging) character, he features in some of the most poignant moments in the book, such as his gift of Nikolai Gogol's stories to his son and the late-discovered inscription in that book. In another poignant moment, Ashoke finally reveals the true meaning behind Gogol's name. When Gogol asks his father if he is a reminder of the accident, Ashoke replies, "You remind me of everything that followed."

The adult Gogol also fondly recalls a time when he was around five and he and his father walked alone to the very tip of Cape Cod. Ashoke's sudden death also acts as a catalyst for his son. Indeed, losing his father causes Gogol to finally appreciate his family and heritage.

Gogol Ganguli

Gogol is the novel's protagonist. He struggles with his identity as both an Indian and an American. As a child, he does not wish to be called by his formal name of Nikhil, but by the time he reaches adolescence, he resents his odd name so much that he legally changes his name to Nikhil when he turns eighteen. He tells the judge he has "always hated" the name. Throughout his life, Gogol had avoided reading the work of Nikolai Gogol: "To read the story, he believed, would mean paying tribute to his namesake, accepting it somehow." Now that Gogol has changed his name, however, he must struggle not only with the duality of his cultural identity but with the duality of his two names. It takes some time for Gogol to "feel like Nikhil." His dual names —one at school, one at home—make him feel like "he's cast himself in a play acting the part of twins." It is also odd to him when his parents visit him at school and call him Nikhil, but it is equally odd when his mother forgets and calls him Gogol. He "feels helpless, annoyed … caught in the mess he's made."

As Gogol matures, he distances himself more and more from his family; he resents their Indianness and provincial lifestyle. He dates Maxine Ratliff, a woman whose family he admires and whose lifestyle he aspires to, yet "he is conscious of the fact that his immersion in Maxine's family is a betrayal of his own," though he is untroubled, even relieved, by this acknowledgment. His seemingly preposterous relief is evident when his parents are unable to reach him at the Ratliff family lake house. This realization makes Gogol feel "that here at Maxine's side, in this cloistered wilderness, he is free."

However, after his father's death, Gogol experiences a change of heart. He breaks up with Maxine, is closer to his family, and makes peace with his heritage. He ultimately marries an Indian American woman. Sadly, Gogol's wife, Moushumi, has not made the same peace with her background that Gogol has, and her constant dissatisfaction destroys their marriage. When he learns of her affair it is "the first time in his life [when] another man's name upset him more than his own." Moreover, the peace that Gogol has made with himself is underscored at the end of the novel when he realizes that "the name he had so detested … was the first thing his father had ever given him." He also thinks that there are only a few people left in his life that know him as Gogol, and "yet the thought of this eventual demise provides no sense of victory, no solace. It provides no solace at all."

Nikhil Ganguli

See Gogol Ganguli

Sonali Ganguli

See Sonia Ganguli

Sonia Ganguli

Sonia is Gogol's sister. She does not appear much in the story, but when she does, she often serves as a contrast to Gogol. As a baby, she is given only one name and is labeled the "true American." Also unlike Gogol, she moves rather far away from her family. However, like Gogol, she returns after Ashoke's death. Sonia marries Ben, an American who makes her very happy.

Moushumi Mazoomdar

Moushumi becomes Gogol's wife. Like Gogol, she is an Indian American. In fact, they attended the same large Bengali parties as children, but they never interacted and only vaguely remember one another. The two are chosen as romantic possibilities by their mothers; to their mutual surprise, they fall in love. Notably, both rejected backgrounds, and both nevertheless resented their American lovers for doing the same. Moushumi, unlike Gogol, has not truly made peace with her background. She still aspires to be like her American college friends. Her disappointment at her failure to achieve that ideal keeps her largely dissatisfied with her life. In fact, it is this dissatisfaction that drives her into the arms of an idealized old flame who has aged badly.

Maxine Ratliff

Maxine is one of Gogol's girlfriends. She lives on a private floor in her parents' mansion in Chelsea (in New York City), and dines with them regularly. Maxine and her family represent the fine American lifestyle to which Gogol aspires. He is comfortable in her world in a way his parents never could be. On the other hand, Maxine is comfortable around Gogol's parents despite Gogol's own embarrassment. Eventually, Maxine's charm wears thin when Gogol becomes more attached to his family. Gogol prefers to retrieve his father's body alone and to mourn with his mother and sister alone. When Maxine urges him to take a vacation and get away from his family's grief, Gogol says that he does not wish to do so. Indeed, Gogol's growing attachment to his family and his exclusion of Maxine lead to the end of their relationship.

Ruth

Ruth is Gogol's first love. He is introduced to her parents and accepted by them, but he does not introduce Ruth to his parents. This is because he knows his parents would rather he date a Bengali girl—or rather, they want him to focus on his studies and date Bengali girls after he graduates. Ruth dates Gogol for a couple of years, even maintaining a long-distance relationship with him while she is studying abroad in England. However, when she returns, she and Gogol agree that they have grown apart, and they break up shortly thereafter.

Topics for Further Study

- Read a short story by Lahiri and compare it to *The Namesake*. In an essay, discuss the similarities and differences in theme and tone between the two works. Lahiri's writing is known for its portrayal of the Indian American experience. How does your reading add to your understanding of that experience?

- Conduct an Internet research project on immigration in the United States during the twentieth century. What statistics can you uncover regarding the immigration rates of Indians over that period? How do the Gangulis' experiences correlate with those statistics? Present your findings to the class using charts and graphs.

- Read "The Overcoat," a short story by Nikolai Gogol, and give an oral book report relating your impressions of it. Be sure to discuss any added insights the story has lent to your reading of *The Namesake*.

- Which character in the novel did you identify with most (or least)? Why? Write a brief essay answering these questions. In the essay, give specific examples from the text showing what makes that character most (or least) like you.

Themes

Immigrant Experience

One of the main themes in the novel is that of the immigrant experience. Ashoke and Ashima are immigrants traveling from the country they have always known to make their life in a vastly foreign land. While Ashoke is able to throw himself into his work, through Ashima readers catch a glimpse of the anxiety and alienation of foreigners. In the first sentence of the novel, Ashima is attempting to make a snack resembling her favorite food back home. However, the attempt is an inexact copy; the original ingredients are unavailable in Cambridge, and Ashima can only effect an approximation. This first image applies to much of Ashoke and Ashima's lives. Their Bengali friends are an approximation of the extended family they left behind. Their attempts to name Gogol according to the Indian tradition of pet names and formal names are misconstrued and ultimately abandoned, another failed approximation. Indeed, even as the years go on, Ashoke and Ashima remain tied to India, visiting it every few years. No matter how long they live in America, they will always be living in a foreign land. This is an essential aspect of Ashoke and Ashima's experience.

The process of assimilation, in which immigrants take on the mannerisms and customs of their new country, is also evident in *The Namesake*. For instance, Ashoke and Ashima begin celebrating Christmas and Easter, though they do so mainly for their children. In fact, Gogol and Sonia, as first-generation Americans, also demonstrate an important aspect of the immigrant experience. As first-generation Americans, they are not living in a foreign land; they are not pulled between two countries in the way that their parents are, but they are pulled between two *cultures* in a way that their parents are not. Indeed, Ashoke and Ashima do not feel the need to conform to American ideals and traditions, yet their children, especially Gogol, do. As children, Gogol and Sonia urge their parents to celebrate Christian holidays, they prefer American food to Indian food, and they resent the long family trips to India. Where their parents entered into an arranged marriage, Gogol and Sonia date Americans freely. Even when Gogol and Moushumi eventually marry, they still prefer an American wedding. Instead, they have a Bengali ceremony to please their families. Gogol, Sonia, and even Moushumi must balance two heritages, the American one they grew up with and the Indian one they inherited. Each does so with varying degrees of success.

Identity

While *The Namesake* largely explores the immigrant experience, it cannot help but touch upon the closely related theme of identity. Indeed, the dual heritages that Gogol, Sonia, and Moushumi carry are essentially two cultural identities. The unasked question that haunts their lives is whether they are Indian or American. The answer is that they are simultaneously both and neither. It would be an oversimplification to say that they are Indian Americans, but this nevertheless speaks not only to the trouble that first-generation immigrants have identifying themselves but also the trouble that outsiders have in identifying bicultural individuals. This quandary is largely represented in Gogol's two names. In fact, Gogol's changing feelings regarding his name correspond to his feelings about his cultural identity. When Gogol accepts the name given him by his parents, it is as if he is accepting them. Notably, when he attempts to create himself anew as Nikhil, he feels torn between two identities, but when he fully embraces his name and his Indian heritage, he does not feel any anxiety. His two names—one at school, one at home—make him feel as if "he's cast himself in a play acting the part of twins." Amidst the confusion he has caused, Gogol "feels helpless, annoyed … caught in the mess he's made."

As the novel progresses, Gogol becomes more comfortable with his Indian identity, with the rituals and customs that connect him to his family. This change enables him to marry Moushumi, to ungrudgingly do so in a ceremony contrary to his personal tastes. By the novel's end, Gogol realizes that "the name he had so detested … was the first thing his father had ever given him." Indeed, by rejecting his name, Gogol had rejected his father, his parents, his roots, and his identity—all things he no longer rejects. Now, having all but succeeded in obliterating his original name, "the thought of this eventual demise provides no sense of victory, no solace. It provides no solace at all."

Omniscient Third-Person Narrator

The use an omniscient third-person narrator in *The Namesake* gives the reader insight into the private thoughts of each of the novel's characters. This narrative device allows the reader to observe both the outer and inner realities of each character. In this way, the reader truly understands the angst and anxiety that are experienced by Ashima, Gogol, and Moushumi, as well as their perceived reasons for those feelings. On the other hand, the omniscient narrator simultaneously acts as a distancing device. If the novel were told from a first-person point of view, particularly from Gogol's perspective, then the reader would identify directly with the narrator's actions. The book would also take on a more conversational tone, as if the reader and the first-person narrator were interacting directly. Instead, the narration becomes somewhat static, matter-of-factly relating Gogol's actions and thoughts over the course of thirty years. Indeed, this approach leaves the reader with a greater awareness of the fact that a story is being told. Thus, the reader becomes somewhat more distanced from the characters' lives and realities, as they are being held at arm's length by the book's narrative approach.

Motif

Originally a musical term, a motif is a thought or idea that appears repeatedly throughout a work. The importance of names and their origins is one of many motifs in *The Namesake*. In fact, it is the force that drives and informs the entire narrative. Indeed, while Gogol's name is a particularly strong motif, motifs in general act to bind together a work, adding continuity and thematic resonance. Another important motif in the novel is that of the train, and even of the train's odd pairing with love and death. For instance, Ashoke's train accident is of obvious significance, and that significance is underscored by Gogol's frequent use of the train to visit with his family. Indeed, Gogol meets his first love on the train, and his marriage also falls apart on the train. When Gogol and his family are traveling by train through India, a man is murdered in another car. When Gogol heads home on the train Thanksgiving break of his senior year, someone commits suicide by jumping on the tracks. This latter incident causes Gogol to be late, and Ashoke sits alone at the station, worrying that the same fate that once befell him may have befallen his son. Indeed, it is Ashoke's relief following this worry that spurs him to reveal the true meaning behind his son's name.

Nikolai Gogol

Russian author Nikolai Gogol was born in Velikie Sorochintsy, in what is now Ukraine, on March 20, 1809. His parents, Maria Ivanovna and Vasilii Afanas'evich Gogol-Ianovsky owned land; though the family was not rich, they were relatively well off. Gogol was the first infant in the family to survive, though Maria Ivanovna and Vasilii Afanas'evich went on to have five more children. Gogol began writing satirical poetry in high school, though he was not a good student. However, after his father died in 1825, Gogol pursued his studies with greater dedication. It was around this time that he began writing longer poems, but few, if any, have survived. In 1828, Gogol moved to St. Petersburg in the hopes of securing employment, but he was sorely disappointed by the low-level civil service positions available to him. He eventually took a poorly paying job that left him with enough time to pursue his writing. In 1829 he self-published the poetry collection *Gants Kiukhel'garten* under the name V. Alov. It received such bad reviews that Gogol burned all of his remaining copies.

That same year, Gogol traveled to Germany for six weeks before returning to St. Petersburg and taking a job in the ministry of the interior. He also resumed his literary career, publishing essays, poems, and historical chapters in various periodicals. Almost all were written under various pseudonyms. He eventually began to attract the attention of literary patrons, including the great Russian writer Alexander Pushkin. Through these connections, Gogol secured a job as a history teacher at the Patriotic Institute for the daughters of the nobility in 1831. At this time, Gogol began collecting family anecdotes related to the Ukraine, most of which comprise his earliest short stories, first published in *Vechera na khutore bliz Dikan'ki* in two volumes in 1831 and 1832. The work established Gogol's reputation as a writer of note.

In 1834, Gogol joined the University of St. Petersburg as an assistant professor in history, but he left in 1835. He also published his second and third story collections that year, *Arabeski* and *Mirgorod*. Both were well received by critics. Over the course of the 1830s and early 1840s, Gogol also wrote several plays, with mixed success. In 1842, Gogol achieved his greatest literary success, releasing the short story collection *Sochineniia*, which includes "The Overcoat," his best-known story. He also published his first and only novel, *Mertvye dushi*, which is best known in English translation as *Dead Souls*. Both works represent Gogol at the height of his prowess. Afterwards, he struggled to write a sequel to his novel and destroyed several versions.

By the late 1840s, Gogol had befriended Father Matvei Konstantinovsky. The priest lambasted the author's work as vain and sinful. Believing Konstantinovsky and fearing for his soul, Gogol stopped writing in 1852. He also began fasting, ultimately starving himself. Despite the efforts of friends and other clergy, Gogol refused to eat, and he died February 21, 1952.

Indian American Immigration in the Late Twentieth Century

Until 1946, Indian and other Asian immigrants experienced greater difficulty entering the United States than their European and Latin American counterparts. This changed to some extent with the signing of the Luce-Cellar Bill by President Harry S. Truman in 1946. The bill was incorporated into the Immigration Act of 1946; it allowed Indians the ability to gain citizenship to the United States. The bill also allowed Indian immigrants to travel back and forth between India and America more freely. At the time, however, only 100 Indian citizens per year were able to immigrate legally to the United States. With the passage of the Immigration Act of 1965, however, this number was expanded to 20,000. This change led to a marked influx in the Indian population in America. Indeed, *The Namesake* begins in 1968, three years after the act was passed. The Gangulis' presence in America, as well as that of the myriad Bengali friends they make, is attributable to this act.

Critical Overview

Given the remarkable success of Jhumpa Lahiri's first book, *Interpreter of Maladies*, the author's follow-up publication was highly anticipated. For the most part, *The Namesake* did not disappoint; like its predecessor, the volume met with wide critical approval. For instance, Michiko Kakutani states in the *New York Times* that the novel "is that rare thing: an intimate, closely observed family portrait that effortlessly and discreetly unfolds to disclose a capacious social vision." Proffering further praise, Kakutani declares that "Lahiri has not only given us a wonderfully intimate and knowing family portrait, she has also taken the haunting chamber music of her first collection of stories and reorchestrated its themes of exile and identity to create a symphonic work, a debut novel that is as assured and eloquent as the work of a longtime master of the craft."

On the other hand, *Commentary* reviewer Sam Munson was less impressed. In his article, he remarks that the tone features "an excess of dispassionateness: Lahiri's novel is linear to the point of monotony." He adds that the book "does occasionally rise to the level of which Lahiri is manifestly capable," but he ultimately finds that "these moments only serve in the end to underline the flatness of the whole." Nevertheless, Munson's opinion is decidedly in the minority. Indeed, *Kenyon Review* contributor David H. Lynn notes that "what Lahiri aspires to is considerably grander than whether readers become emotionally engaged with her characters. Her ambition is to play in the literary big leagues." Mandira Sen, writing in the *Women's Review of Books*, also gives a glowing assessment in her critique. She comments that "Lahiri's beautifully crafted and elegantly written novel will speak to many. It is as different as it can be from the exotic outpourings of Indian immigrants writing in English for whom the home country provides a canvas for their magical interpretations." Furthermore, Sen observes, Lahiri "steers away from providing easy answers, offering readers a complex look into the immigrant experience."

What Do I Read Next?

- Kashmira Sheth's *Blue Jasmine*, published in 2004, is the story of twelve-year-old Seema, who moves from India to Iowa City, Iowa, with her family and struggles to adjust to her new home. This young adult novel presents a another aspect of immigrant experience, this time from the point of view of a young girl.

- For another fictional look at an Indian American who must come to terms with her heritage, read Anjali Banerjee's *Maya Running* (2005). This young adult novel features Maya, a Canadian whose parents are Bengali. Maya experiences the normal teenage angst that accompanies first crushes, but she also must compete with her beautiful cousin Pinky, who is visiting from India.

- Edwidge Danticat's *Behind the Mountains* (2002) also looks at the immigrant experience, this time from the viewpoint of a Haitian refugee. This young adult novel is written as the journal of Celiane, a thirteen-year-old girl who writes about her and her mother and brother's lives in Haiti. Celiane also discusses her new life in Brooklyn, New York, as she and her family travel to join her father there.

- Lahiri's Pulitzer Prize-winning

collection of short stories, *Interpreter of Maladies* launched the author to international fame in 1999. The book will add much to any reading of *The Namesake*, as both volumes explore the Indian American immigrant experience. Both books are also largely autobiographical.

- For more insight into the works of Nikolai Gogol, read his *Collected Tales*. The volume, published in 2008, was translated into English by Richard Pevear and Larissa Volokhonsky. The collection also features the Russian writer's best-known story, "The Overcoat."

- The anonymously authored *India*, released by DK Publishing in 2008, presents a pictorial survey of the country that informs Lahiri's novel. The book also includes text on the customs, religions, and history of India.

- While the Gangulis are not particularly religious, or even identified as Hindus, the rituals they take part in are indeed Hindu customs. For more insight into this fascinating and ancient religion, read *The Essentials of Hinduism: A Comprehensive Overview of the*

World's Oldest Religion (2002), by
Swami Bhaskarananda.

Sources

Adams, Amy Singleton, "Nikolai Vasil'evich Gogol," in *Dictionary of Literary Biography*, Vol. 198, *Russian Literature in the Age of Pushkin and Gogol: Prose*, edited by Christine A. Rydel, The Gale Group, 1999, pp. 137-66.

Friedman, Natalie, "From Hybrids to Tourists: Children of Immigrants in Jhumpa Lahiri's *The Namesake*," in *Critique: Studies in Contemporary Fiction*, Vol. 50, No. 1, Fall 2008, p. 111.

Kakutani, Michiko, "From Calcutta to Suburbia: A Family's Perplexing Journey," in *New York Times*, September 2, 2003, p. E8.

Lahiri, Jhumpa, *The Namesake*, Houghton Mifflin, 2003.

Lynn, David H., "Virtues of Ambition," in *Kenyon Review*, Vol. 26, No. 3, Summer 2004, p. 160.

Munson, Sam, "Born in the U.S.A.," in *Commentary*, Vol. 116, November 2003, p. 68.

Rezaul Karim, "Jhumpa Lahiri," in *Dictionary of Literary Biography*, Vol. 323, *South Asian Writers in English*, edited by Fakrul Alam, Thomson Gale, 2006, pp. 205-210.

Sen, Mandira, "Names and Nicknames," in *Women's Review of Books*, Vol. 21, No. 6, March 2004, p. 9.

Singh, Inder, "Struggle of Indians for US

Citizenship," in *Guyana Journal*, July 2006.

Further Reading

Khandelwal, Madhulika S., *Becoming American, Being Indian: An Immigrant Community in New York City*, Cornell University Press, 2002.

> This book, a nonfiction, anthropological account, provides an excellent overview of the Indian immigrant experience from the 1960s to 2000.

Lahiri, Jhumpa, *Unaccustomed Earth*, Knopf, 2008.

> As of 2009, Lahiri had written only three books. All three explore the Indian American experience, and while they are stand-alone works, their unifying subject matter makes it worth reading them together.

Nabokov, Vladimir, *Nikolai Gogol*, New Directions, corrected edition, 1961.

> This volume is a classic biography of the Russian writer, written by another famous Russian author. It has remained in print for over forty years.

Roy, Arundhati, *The God of Small Things*, Random House, 1997.

> Roy portrays an Indian family living in India during the 1960s in this

contemporary classic novel. The volume provides a nice contrast to Lahiri's portrayal of Indian Americans living in the United Sates.